The Spinning Heart Study Guide 2020

CRACK THE COMPARATIVE #4

Amy Farrell

SCENE BY SCENE
WICKLOW, IRELAND

Copyright © 2020 by Scene by Scene.

Without limiting the rights under copyright, this book is sold subject to the condition that it shall not, by way of trade or otherwise be lent, resold, hired out, reproduced, stored on or introduced into a retrieval system, or transmitted, in any form or by any means (electronic, mechanical, photocopying, recording or otherwise), or otherwise circulated, without the publisher's prior consent, in any form other than that in which it is published and without a similar condition, including this condition, being imposed on the subsequent publisher.

All rights reserved. No part of this publication may be recorded or transmitted in any form or by any means electronic, mechanical, photocopying, recording or otherwise without the proper consent of the publisher.

The publisher reserves the right to change, without notice, at any time, the specification of this product, whether by change of materials, colours, format, text revision or any other characteristic.

Scene by Scene
Wicklow, Ireland.
www.scenebyscene.ie

The Spinning Heart Study Guide 2020 by Amy Farrell.
ISBN 978-1-910949-81-8

Illustration © Polinaraulina

Contents

Understanding the Mode - Cultural Context/Social Setting	2
Notes on Cultural Context/Social Setting	4
Cultural Context/Social Setting - Key Moments	6
Pokey Burke Cheats His Workers	6
Lily is Beaten by her Baby's Father	6
Réaltín Lives in a Ghost Estate	7
Jason Recounts Violence and has a Sexist Outlook	9
Seanie's Sexism, Toxic Masculinity and Depression	10
Denis' Financial Desperation and Violence	11
Understanding the Mode - Literary Genre	12
Notes on Literary Genre	14
Literary Genre - Key Moments	17
Bobby speaks about his life	17
Timmy's Unhappy Upbringing	19
Trevor's Dark Plans	20
Denis' Guilt	21
Frank's Perspective	22
Triona Completes the Narrative	23
Understanding the Mode - Theme/Issue – Relationships	24
Notes on Theme/Issue - Relationships	25
Theme/Issue - Relationships - Key Moments	27
Bobby's Hatred for his Father (Frank)	27
Jason's Relationship with the Mother of his Child	28
Denis and Kate's Loveless Marriage	29
Mags is Shamed by her Father (Josie)	30
Frank Mahon Remembers Being Beaten by his Father	31

Triona's Love for Bobby	32
Understanding the Mode - Hero, Heroine, Villain (OL)	**34**
Notes on Hero, Heroine, Villain (OL)	**35**
Hero, Heroine, Villain - Key Moments	**37**
Bobby's View of Himself	37
Bobby Looks out for Timmy	38
Jason Calls Bobby a Murderer	39
Rory Admires Bobby	39
Frank's View of His Son	40
Triona's Love for Bobby	41

About This Book

This book is a study guide for Leaving Certificate English students sitting their exam in 2020. It provides notes for the Comparative Study of *The Spinning Heart* by Donal Ryan.

There are notes and analysis of key moments for Cultural Context/Social Setting, Literary Genre, Theme/Issue (Relationships) and Hero, Heroine, Villain.

I have selected key moments to analyse for each comparative study mode. However, my choices are not definitive - any moment can be considered and explored for any mode. Feel free to consider other moments to add to your analysis for the comparative study.

'The Spinning Heart' by Donal Ryan

'The Spinning Heart' is set in a rural town in the time after Ireland's financial collapse. The narrative centres on the protagonist, Bobby Mahon, and his troubled relationship with his father.

Understanding the Mode
Cultural Context/Social Setting

Cultural Context/Social Setting refers to the world of the text. Think about social norms, beliefs, values and attitudes.

Consider the following questions to help you understand the Cultural Context/Social Setting of *The Spinning Heart*.

- What time and place is the story set in?

- What are the rules that characters live by?

- What guides characters' behaviour?

- What do characters fear?

- What do characters believe in – religion, power, love, family, wealth?

- What do characters prioritise – family, money, reputation?

- Who holds the power in this world?
  Who is powerless?

- How are the vulnerable members of society treated in this world?
  Are they protected or persecuted?

- Is this a supportive, loving world?

- Is this a harsh, threatening world?

- How does this world impact on characters' lives and relationships?

- How free are characters in this world?

- How controlled are characters in this world?
  Who controls them?
  Who has the power?
  Why do they have this power?
  Why are they obeyed/why are rules followed?

- What strikes you about the society of the text?

- What is the world of this text like?

- What is it like to live here?

Notes on Cultural Context/Social Setting

This story is set within the timeframe of the recent **recession** in Ireland, the period following the **economic collapse** that occurred in 2008. Characters are out of work, with little money or job prospects. This **unemployment** leaves characters feeling ashamed and **frustrated**, and creates an environment where those with work are told to consider themselves lucky to have a job at all.

There is a culture within this world of **men repressing their emotions**, and **reacting explosively when angered**. This takes its toll on the men in the story, for example, Seanie Shaper suffers with depression without reaching out for help, unable to articulate how he is feeling. Similarly, Bobby cannot talk to Triona about what is going on when he is released on bail. **Men suffer in silence** in this society that encourages the repression of men's emotions.

Women in this text are generally wives and mothers, conforming to society's roles for them.

Women also tend to be reduced to sexual objects by the men of this world, described in terms of attractiveness and spoken of in relation to sex. This **sexist outlook** crops up in many chapters: Seanie's, Jason's, Brian's and Rory's for example, suggesting it is widespread in this world.

This is a **violent place**. Jason recounts a shooting, Vasya remembers his brother being beaten to death, and Frank Mahon is killed in his home.

Dylan's abduction adds to the impression that this is an **unpredictable, dangerous place**. Millicent's fear of the Children Snatcher Monster shows the threat the kidnapping represents in this world, where **adults cannot keep children safe**.

There is also a certain **traditional** outlook here, as many characters' parents also lived their whole lives here. This helps create the impression that this is a **close knit community**, where people are well known to one another.

There is a downside to this close knit community. This small town is rife with **gossip, rumour and judgement**. Bobby is rumoured to be having sex with Réaltín because he visits her house to do repair work. He is also assumed to be his father's killer as their terrible relationship is well known. **This is a place where people are quick to jump to conclusions and assume the worst of each other.**

There are also positives to this small town life though. Bridie recounts taking in Bobby and his mother when Frank drunkenly smashed up their home. Her kindness and compassion shows that **goodness and understanding** are also to be found in this place.

There are many **religious** references throughout the text, which shows that religion is very much a part of these people's lives, their culture and this **traditional rural world**. The parish priest is mentioned a number of times, and Frank's chapter ends with him wondering how he will look upon the face of God, making his religious belief very clear. However, this religious aspect of their world does not appear to temper characters' actions or make them any kinder towards one another.

Cultural Context/Social Setting
Key Moments

Pokey Burke Cheats His Workers

The opening chapter details the impact of the **financial collapse** in Ireland.

Bobby recalls how Pokey Burke "shafted" the men who worked for him. Mickey Briars realised that they were not in a proper pension, and **violently challenged** Pokey about it, demanding his pension and stamps.

Unable to get his hands on Pokey, **Mickey could not contain his rage and exploded in anger, violently striking Timmy with a shovel.** This shows **the violent behaviour of men in this world,** and how the innocent are collateral damage, victims of uncontrolled anger.

Bobby remarks that Timmy's injuries do not really matter as you don't need brains to toil on a site and take orders from men who will trick you. This is **not a world where you need to be clever, but one where you need to endure.**

Bobby describes the building site as a **harsh, difficult place** to work, and shows how Pokey has cheated the men who work for him. The **workers are left with nothing** now that they have lost their jobs. **They have no work, no work prospects, and no social welfare payments.**

Lily is Beaten by her Baby's Father

Lily relates being beaten by the father of her baby. While in labour, Lily named the father of her fifth child. **Bernie, outraged to be named as**

the father of a prostitute's baby, **unleashes his anger**, punching her in the mouth and saying he should kill her.

This moment shows the **violence of this world**, where Bernie channels his anger into beating Lily. **His outrage is noteworthy, he resents being known as the baby's father, this slur on his reputation maddens him and provokes this violent assault.**

This attack also shows **how little Lily is worth in this society**, how the **label of prostitute degrades her** and makes Bernie feel that he can treat her like this.

He shows no interest in his child, not wanting anything to do with them. In this world, **Bernie chooses to ignore his unwanted baby.**

The local garda sergeant is relieved when Lily says her injuries are the result of a fall, not wanting to have to follow up on her assault. **Bernie will not be held to account for this assault.**

Lily is scorned and held in disdain in this world. **Her lifetime of sex work makes her vulnerable and isolated.** Now, as an older woman she is entirely alone, forgotten by even her own children, such is their **shame**.

The **judgemental tendencies of this society are clear** in this chapter. Lily is scorned because she has spent her life selling sex to men. She is an unwanted part of the community, someone they would rather ignore. She is a victim of **judgement and violence** in this place that refuses to acknowledge her.

Réaltín Lives in a Ghost Estate

Réaltín's home in a ghost estate perfectly captures the economic

collapse of the recession. Réaltín and her neighbour are isolated and cut-off, living in an estate that was never completed.

The **other houses are unfinished and vacant, demonstrating the sudden financial ruin of the recession.**

Réaltín remembers buying her house and gives us an insight into how **misleading and untruthful** people in this world can be. The auctioneer made Réaltín and her father feel pressure to buy immediately, and that is what they did, eager to secure a home for Réaltín.

Réaltín explains that work ceased on her estate when the builder went bust. She tells us of Pokey Burke, showing how many people in this community were affected by his actions.

These days Réaltín's father cuts the grass and tidies up, **trying to maintain the facade of normalcy**. His love and affection for his daughter is clear. His relationship with his daughter and grandson show that **family love can be strong and positive in this world**.

Réaltín's relationship with Seanie, her son Dylan's father, also gives an insight into this world. Réaltín finds Seanie lacking, saying all he is good for is drinking and shagging floozies. She highlights the **drinking culture** and acceptance of **casual sex** in this world.

Réaltín is not sure if Seanie is Dylan's father, having once had sex with her boss, George. George arranged a night out, hoping that if a girl from the office had enough to drink, she might find him attractive. There is something **predatory** in George's attempts to get young female colleagues drunk and engage them sexually, suggesting a **sexist society**.

Réaltín explains how confused she was during the time she became pregnant by speaking of her mother's death, and her difficulty grieving.

Réaltín carries a private pain and suffering she does not share with others, that has major impacts on her life and happiness.

Jason Recounts Violence and has a Sexist Outlook

Jason's account shows the **difficult, harsh side of living in this world**. He has **a son he never sees** with a woman who has no interest in him.

Jason was abused as a child and has never recovered. He has suffered **trauma** ever since, which has affected his ability to function in society. Jason's story tells us that **children are not safe from predators in this world**.

He also shows how he does not fit into society because of his mental health problems, listing an array of diagnoses he suffers from that he uses to avoid job interviews.

The **violence and unpredictability** of this world is seen when he describes witnessing a shooting. **Jason is a victim of this violent world, his exposure to violence and abuse has impaired his ability to function fully in society.**

This account highlights the **sexism** of this world. Jason speaks about the tattoo artist's assistant as if she is an object, existing for men to look at. He also comments that the apartments given to "slappers" are very nice, using **derogatory language to describe single mothers**.

His own violent tendencies are seen when he says he should have assaulted his son's mother. **Jason, a victim of violence and abuse, is himself violent and abusive in his treatment of others. This suggests a difficult, dangerous world, where characters are unhappy and

quick to lash out.

Seanie's Sexism, Toxic Masculinity and Depression

Seanie's chapter shows us his **sexist views towards women** and the **effects of the culture of toxic masculinity in his society**. He suffers his depression alone, **unable to express how he feels, his sadness, or his feelings of inadequacy.**

Seanie recalls the first time he saw Réaltín. The way she looked at him made him realise how it felt for girls to be ogled and laughed and whistled at by Seanie and his friends. His comment reveals the **casual sexism** of this world and the **toxic masculinity** of Seanie and his co-workers.

Seanie tells us the whole village heard that Bobby was having an affair with Réaltín, showing how **rumour and gossip** are rife in this small, rural community.

Seanie mentions how his family keep secrets out of embarrassment, not wanting to speak about themselves for fear of being judged or looking foolish. He reveals how his culture makes it difficult for him to be open and honest, how **there is a focus on being closed and keeping things to oneself.**

Seanie struggles with his depression alone. He describes how his life has disappointed him, how things have not turned out as he hoped, and how he struggles with this. He **keeps his depression a secret** and cannot bring himself to speak of it. **In this world he cannot be open about his mental health problems.** He allows others to think he is carefree, when in reality he is troubled and depressed. **Seanie secretly suffers his depression, unable to express how he feels in this society.**

Seanie's feelings of inadequacy cause problems in his relationship with Réaltín. He gets mean and nasty with her and cannot express how he wants things to be. He feels that she wants him to be a proper man, and that he falls short. **The emphasis on this macho idea of masculinity is problematic**, it is an ideal Seanie does not feel he can live up to.

Denis' Financial Desperation and Violence

Denis' chapter reveals the pressure and violence of this world in extensive detail. He appears as an isolated figure, suffering from **incredible stress** because of his **dire financial situation**. He is **heavily in debt** and cannot collect what is owed to him, while his wife is only barely tolerating him. Denis is frustrated by his inability to collect the money that he is due, and **his stress and frustration is converted to rage** without any other outlet for it. He talks about driving around the country looking for the men that owe him nearly a hundred grand. He did four or five jobs that he was never paid anything for, and this predicament gives an insight into how **severely he has been affected by the collapse of the building trade**.

Denis speaks of nearly driving over a man in Lackagh, and nearly going through a plate-glass office door in Galway to reach a man who was avoiding him. **In this world it seems, resorting to violence is a response for angry men.**

Denis describes how imagining himself hitting his wife was the only thing that stopped him from actually hitting her.

Denis' search for a link to Pokey Burke, for someone responsible for his situation, is what leads him to Frank Mahon's house. He wanted to scare the old man and make him feel bad about his son, Pokey's foreman. Once again, in this place, bad feeling and hurt leads to further destruction and suffering.

Denis bludgeoned Frank Mahon with a length of wood, imagining himself killing his own father as he did so. In this way Denis highlights a number of aspects of this world, its violence, the frustration and lack of control characters feel due to their economic situation, and the disastrous relationships so many have with their fathers.

Denis' chapter ends with him alone, curled up in bed, tormented by what he has done. His sorrowful state shows us that **despite the violence of this world,** these flawed characters are very emotional and human.

Understanding the Mode Literary Genre

Literary Genre focuses on the ways that texts tell their stories. When analysing Literary Genre, consider the choices the author makes in telling their story this way, and how this impacts on the reader's experience of the story. Think about aspects of narration such as the manner and style of narration, characterisation, setting, tension, literary techniques, etc.

Consider these questions when thinking about Literary Genre.

- How is this story told? (Who tells it? Where and when is it told? How is it structured? What does this add?)

- Why is the story told in this way?

- How does setting add to the story?

- Who is the main character (protagonist)? Do you like them? Why/why not?

- What are the protagonist's main characteristics? Are they an appealing character? Why/why not?

- How does this character change and develop during the course of the story? (character's arc) What causes these changes? Can you plot/chart these changes and developments?

- How does this character interact with other characters? How does this add to the story?

- How are atmosphere and mood created? How do they add to the story?

- Is symbolism used to add to the storytelling?

- How do you respond to the narrative voice?

- Is this an exciting/engaging story? Why/why not?

- Does the author make good use of conflict/tension/suspense?

- What are your favourite moments in the story? What makes these moments stand out for you?

- How does this story make you feel?

- How does it cause you to feel this way?
- Is there just one plot or many plots?
  How do these relate to one another?

- What are the major tensions in the text?
  Are they resolved or not?

- Is this way of telling the story successful and enjoyable?

- Is the story humorous or tragic, romantic or realistic?

- To what genre does it belong?
  Is it Romance, Thriller, Social Realism, Saga, Historical, Fantasy, Science Fiction, Satire?

Notes on Literary Genre

This novel is made up of **twenty-one accounts, each with a different speaker** adding their unique voice to the story. The **protagonist**, Bobby Mahon, **leads the narrative**, with additional characters furthering the action and adding layers of meaning to the reader's understanding of this place and these characters' lives. This **variety of perspectives** builds a richly textured narrative, as plot strands interweave and connections between characters become apparent.

This **sequence of personal accounts** is written in **the vernacular/ demotic**, meaning that it is written in the everyday speech of ordinary Irish people. This gives their stories authenticity and creates a strong sense that these speakers are from this place. This stylistic feature adds to the **auditory**

appeal of the novel; it reads as **a series of spoken accounts** and feels **conversational and personal.**

A feature that each account shares is the speaker's **unburdening** and expression of their **private sorrows, losses and fears**. There is a **confessional feel to the complete honesty and sincerity** that characters express as they bare the **darkest parts of their lives. Characters withhold nothing from the reader** as they admit to failings, flaws and dark deeds they could never speak of, even to their closest loved ones.

Another engaging feature is the **conflict rich nature of the text**. Conflict in the novel adds **excitement, tension** and **reader involvement. Violent outbursts mark the tale**; Vasya's brother is viciously beaten to death, Trevor plans to kill his mother, Denis murders Frank Mahon. Conflict and violence makes the narrative **unpredictable** and **exciting**.

Two distinct plot strands make the novel read almost like a thriller or crime novel. **The murder and kidnapping storylines create suspense and tension** as the reader wonders whether Bobby has killed his father, and worries what will happen to the snatched child. Having to wait for a speaker to broach these exciting topics also adds to the suspense. As each chapter ends the narrative is broken, and the reader must be patient to see how it will resume, another engaging, involving feature of the novel.

The story's **protagonist**, Bobby Mahon, emerges as a good **character**, with many **positive attributes**. He is thoughtful, fair and kind in his treatment of others, he is handsome and athletic, and is a devoted husband. His **vulnerability and sensitivity** further endear him to the reader. It is his fears and worries that make Bobby **relatable**, the reader can identify with how he feels and the struggles he has been through. Bobby is a charismatic, **complex character, privately struggling** with regret and the loss of his mother, and his intense burning hatred of his abusive father.

As characters speak positively and warmly about Bobby, it further confirms him as a good man in the reader's mind.

The author's use of **imagery** creates the impression of this **rural countryside location** and accurately captures this **moment of financial collapse**. The images of Vasya, lost and wandering the fields, Réaltín, alone in her abandoned and forgotten ghost estate, and Denis, frustratedly driving the roads trying to recover money he is owed, create a **vivid picture** of people suffering the effects of the recession, struggling in their daily lives.

Violent images of killing one's father are repeated throughout the novel. Bobby imagines suffocating his father with a pillow, Denis imagines it is his own father he strikes as he kills Frank Mahon, and Frank imagines himself with his hands around his father's throat. **Thoughts of murder are re-visited** over the course of the novel, keeping ideas of negative relationships, and of hating cruel fathers in particular, to the fore of the reader's mind.

There are a number of **exciting moments** that **build tension** and **increase the pace** of the story. Discovering in Jason's chapter that **Frank Mahon has been killed**, and that **Bobby is suspected of the crime**, is a **dramatic high point**. This is a very exciting plot development. It encourages the reader to question Bobby and what we know of him. Also, **the theme of destructive relationships and hateful fathers is made concrete and real by Bobby's alleged actions**.

The **pace increases** in Denis' chapter when he reveals that he has killed Frank Mahon in a violent outburst of rage and frustration. This is a highpoint in the narrative, a very **dramatic moment as the reader witnesses Frank's death** through the killer's eyes.

The final climactic moment occurs in Frank's chapter. The reader finally gets to hear his version of events, which both confirms him as the bitter, twisted, spiteful character he was said to be, while also revealing him as a victim of violence and physical abuse at the hands of his father.

Frank's chapter also **satisfies the reader's curiosity about his murder**, as Frank tells us how he was killed. The issue of Frank's murder and his troubled relationship with his son begins to be **resolved** for the reader. Frank's chapter gives the reader **insight** into how he feels about his son. **In a way, Frank's chapter is what the story has been building towards, it was inevitable that we should hear from this man who has destroyed his son's self belief and caused so much suffering.**

Resolution continues in the novel's final chapter. Triona **resolves unanswered questions for the reader.** She ties up loose ends, telling us that Dylan has been found alive and well, and that Bobby is at home.

Literary Genre
Key Moments

Bobby speaks about his life

The novel opens with a sincere and open account from the perspective of Bobby Mahon, the story's protagonist. **Bobby's feelings of loss and his destructive relationship with his father are at the heart of the novel**, setting the tone and laying the thematic landscape of the text. The narrative in subsequent chapters will overlay the story that Bobby sets up in this first chapter.

The protagonist introduces himself, his problems and his damaged relationship with his father to the reader. **Bobby tells us that he visits his father every day, hoping to find him dead. The damaged nature of their relationship is thus introduced on the very first page.** This relationship is central to the plot, as is the issue of negative parent-child relationships.

Bobby details the economic crash and the impact it had on him and his fellow workers on the building site. **Donal Ryan captures this moment in Irish life**, the collapse of the building trade and the onset of the recession, through the struggles of these characters in this small community. Bobby Mahon says he cannot afford to buy the messages, the grief he feels over his inability to provide for his family is palpable. **This sense of loss and being trapped by economic misfortune is a thread that will continue throughout the text.**

Bobby's love for his wife Triona is clear in this chapter. **His devotion to his wife is one of the positive strands of the story, an example of light in an otherwise dark narrative.** He describes her as his lovely, lovely Triona, opening up about his emotions to the reader in a way he cannot in his life. However, Bobby feels that Triona let herself down when she married him, his love for her is tainted by his feelings of inadequacy. **This will be a common trend amongst these characters, their private, inexpressed feelings of failure.**

Bobby circles back to the topic of his father, saying that he thought about killing him all day yesterday. **Ryan uses repetition to place this relationship at the centre of Bobby's story**, to underline it for the reader and emphasise how Bobby has been hurt by this destructive bond.

The passage where Bobby describes his imagined murder of his father is very **visual**. He pictures placing a cushion or pillow over the old man's mouth, batting down his flailing hands. This **foreshadows Frank's murder**, while simultaneously **creating the impression in the reader's mind that Bobby may be capable of an act like this**. Here Ryan suggests that Bobby's hatred of his father is such that he could kill him, something that will add to the murder plot strand later.

Timmy's Unhappy Upbringing

Timmy begins by talking about Bobby Mahon, adding to the reader's perception of this central character. He relates how Bobby has treated him with kindness, giving him lifts to work.

Timmy adds to our sense of the **setting**, speaking about men emigrating in search of work, and the significance of the Church in his life. His nana lived her whole life a short distance from where she was born, highlighting the traditional side of this rural community.

Timmy talks about his childhood, an account steeped in **sadness**. He and his five siblings were split up and sent to live with different relatives following his mother's death, as his father, an alcoholic, was unable to care for them. He goes on to say that his father does not speak to him, adding to the **theme of negative relationships and failed fathers**.

He speaks about his sister Noreen and her baby who did not live. Timmy had stood watch over the house, hoping to keep death out. His unspoken devotion here will mirror others in this **collection of voices that find it so difficult to express emotion** to those that matter to them.

Timmy talks about doing up his nana's cottage and his brother's desire to sell it and tells us about a job interview that did not go well. There is the sense that Timmy has not, and never will have, anything good of his own, a dark thought that adds to the **atmosphere of suffering, loss and grief**.

Trevor's Dark Plans

Trevor's chapter, with his plans of murder, kidnapping and seduction, makes for exciting reading.

He details his flawed relationship with his mother in his opening pages, describing how she belittles him. Thus the **theme of negative parent-child relationships is continued** in this chapter.

Trevor goes on to talk about Réaltín. His interest in her **sets the reader on edge**, an anxiety that deepens when Trevor imagines violently killing Dorothy, Réaltín's only neighbour. The **tone** darkens as Trevor imagines himself plunging a screwdriver into one of Dorothy's eyes. **The violence depicted is sudden and brutal**. He fantasises that the girl (Réaltín) would run into his arms following this bloody act. This catches the reader's attention, prompting us to wonder at his mindset and what he is capable of. In this way, **an intriguing sense of threat and menace is created**.

His fantasies spiral as he states that he is dying of skin cancer, something he views as his mother's fault. He calls his mother evil, claiming he has seen her black, forked tongue. **His assertions here jar the reader, it is clear that his mental health is compromised**. This turn adds **tension** and excitement to the **unfolding plot**. His plan to kill his mother and Dorothy and kidnap Réaltín's son adds to the novel's **dark, troubled tone**. His sinister plans are compelling for the reader, who needs to know what happens next.

Denis' Guilt

Denis' chapter is full of anger and frustration at his financial situation which contributes to the **setting** and **atmosphere** of the novel. He is heavily in debt and owed a fortune, a situation that makes him feel frustrated and helpless, echoing the plight of other speakers. **This repetition of theme and feeling** helps Ryan perfectly capture and depict this moment of financial collapse in Ireland.

When Denis mentions that he killed a man the reader's curiosity is engaged as we wonder whether he is Frank Mahon's murderer. This is a crucial detail, as **Denis' guilt frees Bobby Mahon from any wrongdoing in the reader's mind.** Denis' admission of guilt provides a **moment of relief for the reader as any doubts we harboured about Bobby are dispelled.**

Denis wanted to frighten Frank, to exert some power over him, but ends up killing him. As he kills Frank he imagines he kills his own father, adding to the **themes of destructive relationships and vicious fathers**. The **description of Frank in his final moments is particularly vivid**, as he laughs at his attacker, awaiting the blow that will kill him. **Frank's spiteful, vicious nature is summed up in his mocking defiance at the point of death.**

This is a **climactic moment** for a number of reasons. The **themes of violence and negative father-son relationships combine** in Denis' violent attack on Frank Mahon, placing them at the centre of the novel. The **murder storyline is also unravelled for the reader, though it is not yet resolved for the text's characters.** Denis' revelation clears Bobby's name, the reader's faith in him and his good character is restored, but we must wait and see what will happen to Bobby next, thus maintaining the plot's **tension**. Denis' unburdening and **admission of murder is both an exciting and a satisfying moment,** as we finally learn what really happened to Frank.

Frank's Perspective

Frank's chapter is noteworthy for a number of reasons. He is one of the darkest, **most disliked characters** in the story, and hearing from his **point of view** makes the reader understand him better, and even sympathise with how he has wasted his life in bitterness and cruelty. It also confirms for us that **Frank is indeed the vicious, cruel character he has been painted to be. Even in death he is quick to put his son down and find fault with all he does.**

The **supernatural aspect** of this account, told from this **ghostly perspective, is an intriguing feature.** It prompts many questions for the reader to mull over regarding the presence of Frank's ghost trapped in the place where he died.

His account of his murder is a dramatic **highpoint** in the story. The reader hears how Frank died in his words, resolving this plot thread.

Frank's perspective also adds to the sense of **sadness and loss** in the novel. He speaks of his father beating him, and wonders how he went on to treat Bobby as he did. There is a sense of inevitability about the way he hurt his son that adds to the **feeling of needless loss and personal grief experienced by the novel's characters.**

By including Frank's chapter despite this character's death, the author has created **a satisfying sense of completion** to the narrative. The absence of Frank's perspective, when he is such a central force in the story, would detract from the text. **His account is placed perfectly here from a structural point of view, helping to finish the tale and satisfy the reader.**

Triona Completes the Narrative

Triona's chapter **completes the narrative** and leaves a lasting impression on the reader. Her love for Bobby comes through strongly in this chapter. Triona's complete devotion to Bobby and understanding of his private sadness is a testament to their relationship, **a very positive contrast to many of the other flawed and fractured relationships in the novel.** She tells us that she would not care if Bobby never brought a cent into their home, nor did she ever consider that he had been unfaithful to her. **Her belief in Bobby is total**, and this faith **re-confirms him as a hero** in the reader's eyes. The entire narrative has been layering an impression of Bobby as a good and true person, someone the reader can believe in, and **Triona's love and commitment is satisfying for the reader**, such is our emotional connection with Bobby.

She adds details about Bobby's terrible relationship with his father, but despite these negative aspects, she creates a sense of hope and possibility for the future through her love for her husband. She says she would not care even if Bobby had killed his father. **Her love and steadfast belief in Bobby are a positive, affirming comment on their relationship, creating a sense of hope and optimism as the story ends.**

Added to this **satisfying ending on an emotional front** is the news in the final section that Dylan has been found alive and well. Our worst fears have been averted, the innocent child has been spared. Thus, **the kidnapping storyline is resolved positively, suggesting redemption and hope. Triona's chapter ties the threads of the story together** giving the story a sense of completion and closure.

Understanding the Mode
Theme/Issue – Relationships

Relationships has been selected as the theme/issue to explore in this text.

The theme of relationships can be applied to any relationship in a text and includes love, marriage, friendship and family bonds. When analysing this theme consider the complexities of relationships and the impact they have on characters' lives.

Consider the following questions to help you explore the theme of relationships.

- Are relationships generally negative or positive in the text?

- How well do characters communicate and express themselves to one another?

- Do characters trust each other?

- Do characters betray each other?

- Do you see conflict in the relationships in this text?

- Do characters love and respect one another?
  What makes them behave this way?

- How do relationships affect the storyline?

- How are relationships affected by the world of the text?

- Do the relationships in this text make life better or worse for characters?
  Do their relationships bring characters joy or sorrow?

- Are relationships complex and complicated?
  What makes them this way?

- Focus on a single significant relationship in the text – is it positive or negative?
  What makes it this way?

Notes on Theme/Issue - Relationships

The relationships in the novel are overwhelmingly negative, destructive and saddening. Few characters, with the exception of Bobby and Triona, experience real love, warmth or support in their lives, but rather are crippled by the effects of damaging relationships. This is a central theme in the novel, **showing the unhappiness that poor relationships can cause in characters' lives.**

Frank Mahon has treated Bobby and his mother with **spite and scorn** throughout his life, eroding their bond as they were afraid to speak around him for fear of accusations and his sharp tongue.

Both as a child and now as an adult, **Bobby's relationship with his father is extremely flawed.** Bobby visits his father every day, physically present in his father's life, but this is **a shell of a relationship, empty of**

warmth or love. In fact, even in death, Frank mocks and belittles Bobby, forever seeing his son's failings.

Frank himself was the victim of an abusive father, who once beat him severely with a length of wavin pipe for boasting about being clever in school. This shows the **prevalence of anger and violence** in the relationships in the story.

Bobby's negative relationship with his father is magnified and amplified by other similar father-son relationships in the text. Denis also speaks of hating his father, while Timmy's father was completely absent, abandoning him and his siblings. **Sons hating their fathers is a recurring idea**. Frank's murder powerfully demonstrates this theme; Bobby is suspected, as their failed relationship and Frank's vicious nature are so well known, but it was actually another man who hated his father that killed Frank. This shows **how common these failed relationships are**, and also **how damaging their effects can be**.

Even when relationships are not marked by violence, many bring sorrow and disappointment to characters' lives, and many experience **loneliness and isolation**. Bridie is a very lonely character, forever affected by her son's drowning, which led to the **breakdown of her marriage**. Seanie Shaper is similarly alone, feeling inadequate and adrift after his **failed relationship** with Réaltín. **Characters struggle with their relationships, hampered by their inability to express themselves emotionally** and really say what is in their hearts.

In this way, **an inability to communicate** is seen to be a common trait in many of these relationships, just as **violence** is. In both cases, these **flaws erode and break down relationships, making characters unhappy**.

A redeeming, positive relationship we see is that of Bobby and

Triona. Bobby loves his wife, just as she loves him. They offer a glimpse of warmth, support and positive emotion that is absent from many of the other relationships in the novel. Threats to their marriage, such as Réaltín's pursuit of Bobby, the rumours that arise regarding Bobby and Réaltín, and the murder charge, are all insignificant by the novel's end, suggesting a strong, committed, loving relationship.

There are **also positive family relationships,** such as Réaltín and her kind, considerate father, and Rory and his respect for his parents.

Theme/Issue - Relationships Key Moments

Bobby's Hatred for his Father (Frank)

The novel's opening paragraph details how Bobby and his spiteful father feel about one another. **Bobby and his father, Frank, have a very negative relationship.**

Bobby tells us that **Frank always found fault** in his son and wife. His account of living with his father shows how bitter and spiteful the older man was and how he lashed out and hurt those around him with his actions and sharp words.

Frank found fault in everything, making Bobby and his mother afraid to do anything or speak freely in front of him. In this way, Frank not only ruined his own relationship with his wife and son, but destroyed the bond between them too, something that fills Bobby with **regret**. Bobby cannot go back and put things right with his mother, her death prevents him from mending their relationship.

Bobby imagines killing his father, picturing himself suffocating the old man. **Bobby wishes for his father's death, giving an insight into how much he despises him, how damaged and dysfunctional their relationship is.**

The lasting impression we get of Bobby's troubled relationship with his father is one of hatred and waste. They are tied together by pain and resentment in a toxic bond that brings only pain. It is worth noting how this negative relationship has impacted on Bobby, causing him sadness, loss and regret.

Jason's Relationship with the Mother of his Child

Jason's account is marked by **negative relationships** and damaging experiences, adding to the negative portrayal of relationships in the text.

He says the biggest mistake he made was getting tattoos all over his face, something he did for a woman. He says he would have done anything she wanted, and acted on her suggestion to get a spider tattooed on his cheek.

Jason describes how this girl wanted to get pregnant by him, and then wanted him for little else. Jason says he **only saw his son once**. He clearly **feels rejected** by this girl whose child he fathered.

Jason too is a victim of negative relationships. He deals poorly with his sadness and feelings of rejection. He tells us that he should have burst through the door and slapped the head off his son's mother when she would not let him into her home to see his son. **Like other frustrated, angry characters in the novel, he feels resorting to violence is the way to**

get what he wants.

Jason is a victim of sexual abuse, violence and destructive relationships, and has been traumatised and damaged by his experiences. He mentions many interactions and **relationships that damaged him** in some way: the girl who only wanted to get pregnant and then cut him out of her life, the neighbour who sexually abused him, the culchie who shot someone in front of him. **Jason's account highlights the damaging effect of destructive relationships and the huge impact they have on those subjected to them.**

Denis and Kate's Loveless Marriage

Denis and Kate's marriage appears to lack love and understanding. As his chapter begins, Denis is curled up in the foetal position, lying in bed for days. His wife offers him no comfort though, he says she is only **barely tolerating him** and is very close to telling him to cop on and pull himself together. He realises how his wife feels about him, and **the disdain she holds him in.** There is **no warmth or concern** on Kate's part, Denis appears to be suffering alone.

Denis does not seem to feel positively towards his wife either. **His money troubles have added stress and anxiety to his relationship** with Kate, making them **at odds with one another.** He describes picturing himself giving Kate a punch in the mouth, saying imagining this violence was the only way he could stop himself from actually doing it. This **violence and anger directed towards his wife** suggests a serious flaw in their relationship.

Denis goes on to say that **Kate does not know him,** or his thoughts. She does not realise that he is filled with rage, or that he feels so violently towards her. This **gulf between them**, this lack of understanding, is a **negative comment on their marriage**, just as Denis' violent feelings are.

By the end of his chapter it seems that Kate does not know that Denis has killed a man. He hides his crime from her. Denis is suggesting that **his wife does not know the man she is married to** at all, a very negative comment on their relationship. It also adds to the sense that he is very **isolated and cut-off**, dealing with his fears and guilt entirely **alone**.

Mags is Shamed by her Father (Josie)

Mags and her father have a relationship that **lacks closeness or understanding**. She describes how **distant** they are with one another, a gap that cannot be closed.

She imagines sneaking out to listen to him talking to his chickens, knowing that this would embarrass him and that he would be unable to talk to her about it. **She imagines a better version of their relationship**, one where he could put his arm around her and chat to her the way he does with his son and niece and nephew, knowing this can never be the case.

Mags recounts being **ridiculed by her father** at a dinner party. He can no longer love her as he once did. Now that he knows she is a lesbian **he feels ashamed of her**. His prejudice and lack of understanding hinders Josie's ability to treat his daughter as she needs him to, leading to a **disintegration of their once loving bond**.

At this moment, when he hurts her most, Mags wishes for the father from her youth to kiss her forehead and brush her hair back from her forehead. There is sadness in this fond memory, and in **Josie's inability to be the loving father that Mags needs**.

He cannot accept her and love her, caught up in his own prejudices and homophobia. This is another example of **a flawed relationship that causes unhappiness**, adding to the theme of **damaged and hurtful relationships, where those that should love most, deeply fail their loved ones**. Josies lets Mags down when he shames her in front of guests and fails to be the father that she needs. She closes her chapter wishing that he could remember how he loved her, clinging to the memory of her loving father from childhood.

Frank Mahon Remembers Being Beaten by his Father

Frank Mahon's account of being viciously assaulted by his father sheds some light on his character and relationships with his family. It seems that **Frank was himself a victim of violence and cruelty**, something he never managed to overcome, becoming in time a version of his own cruel, hurtful father. **He is a product of destructive relationships**, sadly continuing this cycle of anger and hurt.

Frank relates how he was beaten with a length of wavin piping by his father as a boy. He rushed into the milking parlour to tell his father how clever he was in school, but instead of praise, Frank received a beating. He had got every question right while the cigire visited his school, something his teacher was delighted about. However, instead of taking pride in his son, Frank's father was enraged. He beat the boy with the piping, knocking him flat onto the mucky ground and shouting at him that he knew nothing.

Frank's youthful pride and innocence was met with violence and cruelty, an episode that had a lasting effect on Frank and contributed to his hatred of his father. **This moment in the story showcases negative relationships and their lasting impact, showing how the abuse Frank suffered** helped shape his own destructive relationships with others. This moment also adds to the idea of **negative father-son relationships** and how harmful these relationships can be.

During his drinking days, **Frank used to imagine himself strangling his father**, choking the life from him. These **violent, emotional images** add to our understanding of the force of his **hatred for his father** and this destructive, hateful relationship.

Frank's recollection of being beaten by his father brings the issue of negative relationships to the fore. It shows how negative relationships affect characters and hinder their ability to be happy and forge positive relationships of their own.

Triona's Love for Bobby

Triona's view of Bobby and the love she has for him shows a very positive side to relationships in the novel. Triona loves Bobby and admires who he is.

Triona remembers the first time she spoke to Bobby, and how from that moment on she was wrapped up in him. Her certainty and devotion here are very positive, showing how strongly she feels about him. This **depth of steadfast feeling is a feature of their marriage**. In the Cave bar Triona became aware of Bobby's fear, doubt, shyness and sadness. **Her deep understanding of Bobby and her total acceptance of him are very positive aspects of their relationship.**

Triona's love for Bobby is unconditional. She tells us she would not care if he never earned another penny, his traditional role of provider is not important to her. She also does not care about the rumours about

Bobby having an affair, knowing that he would never betray her. Triona has **complete faith** in her husband.

Triona goes on to say that she would not care if Bobby had killed his father. **There is no judgement here, just love and support**.

Her chapter matches Bobby's earlier one in the positive way she speaks about her spouse. **Their marriage demonstrates mutual love, understanding and support,** and their **commitment** to each other and **certainty of their love** makes it the **most positive relationship in the text**.

Triona understands how Bobby has been hurt by his father. Her compassion is a positive aspect of their relationship.

However, **their marriage is not perfect**. It is marred by **Bobby's inability to communicate freely and openly** with Triona. Bobby cannot speak properly with Triona when he is released on bail. She screams at him to please talk to her. **An inability to communicate openly is a flaw in their marriage, but it does not lessen Triona's love for her husband**. Like the novel's other relationships, theirs is **complex and complicated**, but here we see real **love and understanding** without a shadow of the bitterness and hate of so many other relationships in the text.

Understanding the Mode
Hero, Heroine, Villain
(Ordinary Level)

'Hero, Heroine, Villain' refers to studying central characters (protagonists/antagonists).
Their traits, values, etc. and their ability to deal with conflict, challenges, obstacles, etc. should be considered.
Think about a character's personality, their behaviour, what you like and dislike about them, etc.

Focus on a single character as you consider the following questions:

- Is this character a 'good' main character?
  Are they interesting?
  Are they likeable?
  Do you care about what happens to them? Why/why not?

- What problems and difficulties do they face?
  Do they find facing these problems easy?

- What does this character struggle with?

- What are they good at?

- What makes this character happy?

- Do you feel sorry for this character at any point? Why/why not?

- What sort of life has this character had?

How has this affected them?

- Describe this character's personality.

- What is important to this character?

- If you had a conversation with this character, what would you talk about?
  What advice would you offer them?
  Do you think they would be an easy person to talk to about their problems? Why/why not?

- Do you like this character?
  What makes you feel this way?

Notes on Hero, Heroine, Villain (Ordinary Level)

Bobby Mahon is the story's **protagonist (lead character)**. He opens the novel with his **personal and honest account of his hatred of his father, his grief over losing his mother, details of his working life and his sincere love of his wife. He emerges as a sensitive, thoughtful figure, resentful of his father, but morally sound and kind in his dealings with others.**

Bobby **feels inadequate and foolish** because of how Pokey Burke treated him. When Triona comforts him he feels that she let herself down by marrying him. This shows that **he thinks highly of his wife**, but also that **he feels that he is not good enough**, calling himself useless. **His** feelings of inadequacy add depth and complexity to his character.

Other characters speak highly of Bobby, showing he is respected and admired in his community. Timmy describes him as the only one who never slagged him, and describes Bobby as a kind, thoughtful man. Réaltín emphasises how **handsome and good-looking** he is, while Rory adds to the idea that Bobby is a **natural leader**, a man of action. **The positive way others think of Bobby adds to the sense that he is a good man, who treats people decently.**

Bobby mentions that **he was as smart as any of the posh lads in school, but that he was savvy enough not to show it and be made fun of. This suggests he understands his world and how it works.**

The rumours about Bobby having an affair and killing his father test our faith in him. Rory and Triona disprove the affair, while Denis' admission of murdering Frank clears him of wrongdoing in our eyes. In this way, **our faith in Bobby proves to be well placed.**

Bobby's vicious, mean-spirited father has had a huge effect on Bobby's life, ruining Bobby's relationship with his mother, and causing him much sadness and suffering. **He hates his father** and thinks about killing him, although he is not the one who kills the old man. **The hatred he bears towards his father makes Bobby very real and human.** He is not simply a 'good' character, but a complex one, who has suffered and struggled. This makes him very realistic and believable, and as readers, we care about his story.

Hero, Heroine, Villain Key Moments

Bobby's View of Himself

Bobby's chapter creates the impression that Bobby is a **thoughtful, hard-working character who tries to do what is right**. He feels **frustrated and anxious about his future** now that he has lost his job as foreman.

Bobby gives us an insight into his **feelings of inadequacy** when he talks about how he was treated by Pokey Burke. He feels stupid for being taken in by Pokey Burke and feels he let his wife down. He says his wife Triona pretends not to blame him for being taken for a fool.

Bobby says Triona let herself down when she married him, she could have had any man she wanted. Now he cannot afford to buy groceries. **Bobby is distressed about his lack of income**, and Triona consoles him and reassures him. **He cannot find the words to talk to her** properly, and scolds himself for this, giving himself a hard time for his flaws and failings. **His fears and worries make him a very realistic, relatable character**.

Bobby's **hatred of his father** is very clear in this chapter. In the opening paragraph he tells us he visits his father every day in the hope of finding him dead. Later on he says he spent all of the previous day thinking about killing his father. This hatred is due to Bobby's destructive relationship with his father and the cruel way his father treated Bobby and his mother. **Bobby's backstory shows how difficult his upbringing was** and how he has suffered because of his father. It also shows the **grief and loss** he bears as a result of his father destroying Bobby's relationship with his mother.

Bobby is a troubled character, frustrated by his current situation and lack of work and full of hate for his bitter father. Bobby also shows himself to be a **warm and loving** character when he speaks of his wife and how much he loves and values her. However, he feels he has let Triona down by being taken for a fool by Pokey Burke. His **feelings of inadequacy** and inability to communicate openly with Triona hinder his marriage, despite the deep love he has for his wife.

Overall, Bobby emerges as a thoughtful, complicated character. He is loving and kind, yet he bears a powerful hatred for his father. His character is complex which makes him very real and relatable.

Bobby Looks out for Timmy

Bobby's kindness towards Timmy, a vulnerable character, highlights **Bobby's good nature.** Timmy speaks very highly of Bobby, calling him sound and saying he is the only one of the men who never made fun of him. Bobby used to give Timmy a lift to work, and when Timmy was hit with a shovel it was Bobby who picked him up and asked if he was alright.

Bobby was also the one who **stopped Seanie Shaper from making a laughing stock of Timmy** by showing him a magazine with pictures of naked women and laughing at him with the other men. Bobby threw the magazine into a fire in a tar barrel and told Seanie to leave the boy alone. Here we see **Bobby standing up for someone weaker than him**. Timmy says Seanie was afraid of Bobby when he was in a temper, showing that he is not someone to push around.

Timmy wonders what he will do now for work and says how much he would like it if he could work for Bobby. He says he would work like a dog for Bobby, happy to devote himself to such a man.

In Timmy's account **Bobby emerges as someone who looks after those who are weak or vulnerable.** He appears as someone who cares and **consistently does the right thing, a natural leader.**

Jason Calls Bobby a Murderer

Jason shakes the reader's faith in Bobby, by telling us that Bobby Mahon has killed his father.

Jason forces the reader to consider what we know of Bobby Mahon, and to think about whether he has committed this crime.

As Jason's chapter ends he returns to the topic of Bobby Mahon, calling him 'fair sound'. Bobby tried to give him a job once, thinking he was doing Jason a favour, but Jason called out to Bobby's home to refuse the offer of work. Bobby thanked Jason for letting him know. Then Bobby spotted the buckled front wheel on Jason's father's car and replaced it for him. He is **genuinely kind** here, **doing a good turn and expecting nothing in return**, a gesture that adds to the reader's sense of Bobby as a good man.

Rory Admires Bobby

Rory's chapter is full of **praise for Bobby**. Rory talks about the prospect of working with Bobby, saying how delighted he was when Bobby talked to him about it.

Rory's parents are also delighted that Rory may work for Bobby, viewing him as a **leader** and **man of action**, the type of person who can turn things around from their current grim state. Rory's father says it will be the likes of Bobby Mahon that put an end to the downturn, they have great hope and faith in his ability.

Rory brings up Bobby's alleged affair with Réaltín, but dismisses it totally, saying that **Bobby is completely faithful**.

He then goes on to say that Bobby has murdered his father. Interestingly, Rory does not comment on the murder as being a terrible crime, rather, he says that Frank was a twisted character and that Bobby must finally have had enough of him. **Rory does not pass any negative judgement on Bobby at all**, rather he laments that now he will not be able to work with him because of the murder case.

Rory sees Bobby as someone who is capable and motivated, able to do everything necessary to set up his own business. Rory even says that when faced with a difficult decision, rather than asking himself what Jesus would do, he considers how Bobby would react. This suggests that Rory admires Bobby and thinks he has great judgement.

Frank's View of His Son

Frank's chapter gives insight into Bobby's troubled relationship with his father and his unhappy upbringing.

When Bobby discovered Frank's body, Frank stood beside him and called him a good man. This is high praise from a man who struggled to say anything positive about his son when he was alive. It tells us that **Frank recognised Bobby's goodness, even if he never spoke of it in life**.

Frank's chapter is also full of snide comments about Bobby. He calls him vain, a lapdog of Pokey Burke's and says he is without a dust of sense. Frank's **nasty remarks** and slurs here add to the reader's understanding of **how difficult Bobby's life has been because of Frank**. We realise how constantly negative Frank has been.

Frank says Bobby did not protest his innocence when Jim Gildea, the garda, asked if Bobby had killed his father. Bobby answered that he didn't know, showing **how confused he is by what has happened and his feelings towards his father.** Frank calls Bobby a 'stupid prick' for failing to clear his name. He mocks his son and calls him stupid, blind to the emotional state Bobby is in. Clearly, **Bobby is deeply affected by his father's murder** and is struggling to make sense of it. Frank does not consider how Bobby may be feeling at all.

Frank says he could never talk to Bobby without upsetting him, giving insight into Bobby's sad childhood and difficult relationship with his father. Frank's account adds to the empathy the reader feels towards Bobby, realising **how hard his life has been because of his father.**

Triona's Love for Bobby

Triona's account is full of love and admiration for her husband. She holds him in high regard, never doubting him, but steadfast in her belief of his goodness.

Triona describes Bobby as being different to other men, **someone special** who is not part of the herd. She describes recognising the fear, doubt, shyness and sadness behind his eyes and falling in love with him as a result. Reading her account, it is clear that he is a **sensitive character** and a **deep thinker.**

She also adds to our understanding of Bobby's life growing up, speaking of the coldness of it, and how it hurts Bobby to speak about it. In this way, Triona adds to our understanding of the **trauma and pain Bobby has**

suffered because of Frank.

Triona describes how people look up to Bobby, adding that he is a **natural leader**. Her belief in him, and disregard for the rumours about him, reinforces our sense of Bobby's goodness.

She tells us that Bobby is blind to the effect he has on people, that he does not realise how much people look up to him. **Her view of her husband is overwhelmingly positive**, she recognises the pain in him and accepts and loves it as much as his goodness and strength. Triona adds to the impression that **Bobby is a troubled character, with great depth, compassion and kindness.**

www.ingramcontent.com/pod-product-compliance
Lightning Source LLC
Chambersburg PA
CBHW031546080526
44588CB00018B/2722